I0554679

A Journey Through

the Evidence of Islam

and the Holy Quran's

Divine Origin

Here's Why You Should Convert to ISLAM

From The Sincere Seeker Collection

Copyright © The Sincere Seeker 2023

All Rights Reserved

TABLE OF CONTENTS

WHAT IS ISLAM
IN A NUTSHELL?

Before we speak about the evidence of Islam and the Holy Quran's Divine origin, let me quickly introduce Islam. Islam is defined as the voluntary act of submitting yourself to God. When you become a Muslim, you submit and surrender to the will of God, just as the creation around you, providing you peace and contentment in this life and the hereafter. Only when you submit to God, through a process of believing in Him and obeying His commandments, do you achieve an innate and lasting sense of security, true peace of mind, and surety of heart. As a Muslim, you don't live to fulfill your desires, lusts, and impulses; instead, by definition, a Muslim submits their will to the almighty God. You acknowledge and trust that God knows what's best for you, so you follow His guidance.

You cannot live peacefully or successfully without religion, and this religion cannot be man-made. Religion must be utterly Divine, with no human alteration inherent. The only Revelation in the world today that still rings good and true is the final Book, the last and final Testament of God, the Holy Quran. All other traditional Revelations have been lost in the annals of time or undergone endless human-made modifications that have rendered them impractical for humanity. Unlike other sacred

1

scriptures such as the Bible, the Holy Quran has been perfectly preserved in both its words and meaning—and in a language that still exists today.

Islam is a monotheistic faith that requires followers to admit and recognize the existence of one Supreme God and Being who is Almighty, All-Powerful, All-Knowledgeable, All-Seeing, All-Hearing, Most-Merciful, and Loving. Islam stresses the existence of only One God. The same God worshipped by Prophet Adam, Noah, Abraham, Joseph, Moses, David, Solomon, Jesus, and Prophet Muhammad, peace be upon them all. Islam demonstrates the fact that, through the centuries, God has continued to bless humanity with holy Prophets bearing the same general message.

The message is simple: you should worship God Alone with no partners, love Him with all of your heart, and follow His Commandments. If you follow this edict, you will live a content life in this world and enter Paradise eternally in the afterlife. If you do not believe in God and follow His commandments, you will live a depressed life and enter hellfire in the afterlife.

Islam is not a religion solely based on creeds, customs, and rituals such as praying and fasting; instead, Islam is a complete way of life that guides followers in every aspect of their lives. Islam teaches the art of living and dictates how you should steer and navigate your life. Islam instructs you about the things in this life that are beneficial to you and those that are ultimately destructive and should be avoided.

Islam states that everyday human acts, such as eating, drinking, greeting others, sitting, learning, dressing, sleeping, and giving charity, are all acts of worship if conducted for God alone and in accordance with His Divine Laws and guidelines.

WHO IS ALLAH?

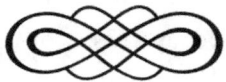

And before we speak about the evidence of Islam and the Holy Quran's Divine origin, let me quickly introduce your Creator to you. Muslims do not worship a particular God of Muslims; instead, the God that Muslims worship is the universal God who created the heavens and the Earth, which many people believe in from the time of their childhood. The word "Allah" is the unique name of God and translates to mean God. Regardless, some people harbor the mistaken belief that Muslims worship a different God than Christians and Jews do and that "Allah" is the God of the Arabs or the Muslims. This is far from the truth.

Arabic-speaking Jews and Christians use the same name, "Allah," to refer to God. If one were to examine an Arabic translation of the Bible, one would see the word "Allah" being used in place of the term, God. However, Muslims, Christians, and Jews have different concepts of God.

Allah is the one and only absolute and eternal God. He is the Creator of the Heavens and Earth, the Creator of the Universe. He is the Lord of all lords and King of all kings. He is the Most Compassionate and Most Merciful. Allah Neither Begets nor is He Begotten. And He knows no equal.

Say, "He is Allah, who is One, Allah, the Eternal Refuge. He neitherbegets nor is born, nor is there to Him any equivalent." (Quran 112:1-4)

Muslims believe in one unique, incomparable God—one with no son, daughter, father, mother, family, or partner. He is the Knower of the unseen and the Source of All Mercy. He is the Creator, the Maker, the Fashioner, the Wise. All that is in the Heavens and on Earth magnifies Him. Muslims believe that none should be worshipped but Him alone. He is the true God, and every other deity is false. None carries the right to be worshipped, revered, adored, invoked, supplicated, or shown any act of worship but Allah alone.

God is unique, indivisible, and similar to nothing. Whenever you try to compare God to anything in this world, the source of comparison cannot be God because God, to put it simply, is incomparable. Your finite human mind cannot comprehend and grasp God as a concept. Muslims avoid conceptualizing His image because imagining or visualizing Him would limit Him. The human imagination is limited, as it is based on what it observes and experiences directly. The human imagination cannot fully grasp God's state, which is timeless and eternal with no beginning or end. God has a unique nature and is free from gender and human weakness. He is beyond anything which human beings can imagine.

"There is no god but He, the Creator of all things; then worship Him, and He has the power to dispose of all affairs. No vision can grasp Him, but His grasp is over all vision; He is the Sublime, Well-Aware." (Quran 6: 102-103)

God is the King, the Holy, free from all defects, The Protector, the Keeper, the Sustainer of Earth and the Universe and all it contains. He is the Glorious, the Great, the deserver of all Praise. The Kingdom of the Heavens and the Earth belong to Him. Nothing is hidden from Him, and nothing is beyond His capabilities. He is the One that merges the night into the day and the day into the night. He is the Master of the Day of Judgment. Allah does not sleep nor slumber, nor does sleep overtake Him.

"He is Creator of the Heavens and the Earth. He has made for you from yourselves, mates, and among the cattle, mates; He multiplies you thereby. There is nothing like unto Him, and He is the Hearing, the Seeing." (Quran 42:11)

God is Loving, Compassionate, and Merciful; He is the answerer of prayers. He is indeed involved and concerned with the daily affairs of all human beings. God is the Beneficent, the Merciful. He is the Giver of life and the Causer of death. He is the Master of the Day of Judgment. He is the Most-High, the Most-Supreme.

God created all things from nothing. He does not need His creation, although His creation needs Him. He is all Knowledgeable and encompasses all things: the open and the secret, the public and the private. He knows all the secrets that lie hidden in the hearts and minds of men. He knows all that happened in the past, what is happening now, and what will happen in the future. Our Lord neither errs nor forgets. He is free from all defects and imperfections. He is the One that accepts repentance from His servants and forgives all sins. Allah knows what you endure and understands your feelings and struggles. Allah understands because He was there with you all along.

Allah has power over all things. No other power, might, strength, or influence can cause benefit or harm to anyone or anything except that which flows through Him. Nothing can happen unless God wills it so. God can make anything happen.

"Not a leaf falls but that He knows it. And no grain is there within the darkness of the earth and no moist or dry thing but that it is written in a clear record." (Quran 6:59)

"Whenever We will anything to be, We say unto it Our word "Be," and it is." (Quran 16:40)

Some people assume that God is a harsh, stern, cruel God who demands to be respected, worshipped, and obeyed fully. They assume He is not loving and kind to His creation. Nothing could be further from the truth. God is All-Loving. He claims among His Names Al-Wadoud in Arabic (the Loving One). The love of God in the Holy Quran is expressed and emphasized many times throughout His Book. God bespeaks His love for the righteous, the charitable, the steadfast, the doers of good, the just, the fair, the benevolent, those who trust Him, the ones that are clean, the ones that purify themselves, and the ones who fulfill their obligations.

The entire Universe contains proof of Allah's love for all of His creation. God gives, without measure, to His servants. He gifted you with life and the ability to hear, feel, taste, and see. God gifted you your heart, mind, soul, strength, and skills. He loves you so much that He gave you an endless variety of foods to feast on, a vast array of land and wildlife, the sun, the moon, the stars, family, offspring, and much more. Everything you see, feel, hear, taste, and smell are blessings given to you by our Loving Creator. He didn't have to create these miracles, but He chose to bestow these blessings upon you. His boundless mercy encompasses everything.

"And He gave you from all you asked of Him. And if you should count the favor of Allah, you could not enumerate them. Indeed, mankind is [generally] most unjust and ungrateful." (Quran 14:34)

God is also All-Just. Hence, evildoers and sinners must be held accountable for their actions. God is holy, righteous, and fair. If He didn't punish evil, He would allow that evil to exist without consequences. Since God cannot allow that to happen, His justice requires that a proper punishment be incurred and executed for evil sins. Although Allah is not answerable to anyone, He has promised to be Just and Fair to everyone.

He has prohibited injustice against the innocent. Allah never would punish an innocent person nor hold anyone accountable for the sins of another. Unlike Christianity, Islam imposes no burden on the original sin. Every human being is born with a clean slate and is rewarded or punished based only on one's willful intent, words, and deeds. Allah is the Absolute Judge, the Legislator. God is the One who distinguishes right from wrong. God even is more merciful to His creation than a mother is to her child. God is far removed from the blight of injustice and tyranny. He is All-Wise in all His actions and decrees.

When you genuinely ponder the Majesty of Allah, your humility increases. You are advised to study and ponder His Names and Attributes and are encouraged to worship and call Him by those names. God states:

"And to Allah belong the best names, so invoke Him by them."
(Quran 7:180)

God is close to those who believe in Him and answers their every call. Nothing is hidden from Him regarding what His creation does or says. He knows all. Saying God is with His servants does not mean He intermingles or dwells with His creation; instead, He establishes His presence through His Knowledge and Power. God is above the heavens and above His Throne. God is outside of His creation. He never is contained by any physical dimension. God states in the Quran:

"Verily, Allah knows all the hidden things of the Heavens and the Earth; Verily He has full Knowledge of all that is in (men's) hearts." (Quran 35:38)

He sees and knows every aspect of His creations. He hears every word uttered. He is even knowledgeable of one's inner thoughts. God knows all of our dreams, secrets, desires, and wishes. Nothing is hidden from Him.

"We created man, and We know what his own self whispers to him. We are nearer to him than his jugular vein." (Quran 50:36)

Allah does not need you, although you do need Him. Allah wants you to worship Him for your own benefit. You need God in your life at all times and for every purpose. When you recognize the Majesty of the Creator of All, you will become awestruck and humble in your response. Rejecting God and His Guidance is like a patient refusing their doctor's medicine to remedy their pain. You will be foolish, ignorant, and illogical if you reject Allah. Allah is Fully Omnipotent and Self-sufficient. He is in no need of humanistic worship or anything else.

Allah is Perfect.

IRREFUTABLE PROOFS AND EVIDENCE ON WHY ISLAM IS THE TRUE RELIGION OF GOD

Many reasons justify the belief that Islam is the religion of God and that the Holy Quran is the true word of God. If you are still unsure of it, you should investigate the evidence that points to Islam as the true faith and that the Holy Quran is the true Speech of God. Let's quickly go over a few of these:

Many proofs exist to support the fact that Islam is the true religion of God. Among the many proofs of Islam's truthfulness is the fact that it is the only religion whose message and teachings have been preserved and never tampered with nor changed over time. As for Christianity and other religions, their original Revelation and teachings have not been preserved for our perusal. If you look at Christianity, for instance, since Jesus Christ and the disciples spoke Aramaic, Jesus Christ's Message and teachings must have been conveyed in that language. Today, we do not have copies of Jesus Christ's teachings available in the language he taught them.

Amongst the many proofs of Islam's truthfulness is that Islam speaks to the predisposition and innate belief God has placed in the hearts of every human. Take the concept of God, for instance. The idea of God is simple, understandable, and not as complex as it is in other religions. Islam teaches the existence of only One Supreme Being, who is All-Mighty, All-Powerful, All-Knowing, All-Seeing, and Most-Merciful, and who created the entire universe and everything in it. All other beings are creations of God and not the actual Creator. If more than one God existed, there would befall a chaos of gods fighting each other for control. If the gods did not fight each other for power and control, then they would be considered dependent on and submissive to each other—in other words, not gods at all.

Among the many proofs of Islam's truthfulness stands the idea that salvation makes common sense and applies true justice. Islam states that salvation is based on believing in your Creator, intentions, actions, and repentance. No other religion supports the belief in rational and logical concepts like Islam's concept of God; thus, the ideas of His Prophets, salvation, and the Hereafter appeal to everyone!

Islam says that every man is responsible for his actions, sins, and salvation; no one will bear the effects of anyone else's sins, as Christianity believes, which is unjust! God, who owns everything, does not need to sacrifice his supposed son to forgive humanity's sins! Moreover, salvation is not based on one's native ethnicity and civilization, over which people have no control, as Jews believe. Where is the fairness, logic, and justice in that?

Islam's concept of the Hereafter makes total sense and applies full justice in its scope. Islam states that there is a life after this one, where everyone will be judged based on how they lived. Everyone will get what they deserve on Judgment Day, be it a reward or a punishment. In this world, evil people may live decent lives and go unpunished for their wrongdoing, while sometimes good people who believe in God and do good deeds live difficult lives. On Judgment Day, justice will be applied.

Among the many proofs of Islam's existence is how its teachings guide you to achieving goodness. Other religions teach you to refrain from stealing and cheating, but their teachings are not practical. In contrast, Islam's teachings are very practical and provide solutions for all problems and aspects of life. Islam offers many resolutions, like the solution to poverty. The faith contains a system known as Zakat, which requires everyone with more than a certain amount of money and assets to give the poor 2.5% of their wealth annually. If everyone followed this system worldwide, no one would die from hunger, and poverty would perish!

Among the proofs of Islam's truthfulness, the most prominent one is the miracle of the Holy Quran. Many reasons exist to justify the truth that the Holy Quran is the true Speech of God. Before we review the evidence that points to the Holy Quran as the Word of God, let's quickly look at the substance of the Holy Quran.

WHAT IS THE HOLY QURAN IN A NUTSHELL?

To navigate humanity to Him, God the Almighty sent down Books with His Prophets to teach and show humankind how to live their lives pleasingly in His eyes—a way of life that delivers contentment in this world and the next while avoiding punishment in the afterlife and attaining Paradise. God sends these Books to serve as study guides and instructional manuals regarding how one's life should be lived. Through his Revelations to humanity, delivered with Prophets, God reveals His Wisdom, Laws, and Instructions.

The Holy Quran is a guide or instructional manual that teaches one how to live their life. The Book was revealed to guide humanity through every aspect of life. The Holy Quran is a personal guide meant to navigate a person through daily struggles. Just as when you buy a computer or any electronic device, the machine comes with an instructional manual dictating its operation.

The Holy Quran deals with all subjects pertaining to the lives of human beings, such as doctrine, wisdom, worship, law, transactions, and more. Its central theme is the relationship between God and His creation. The Holy Quran also teaches the art of living. The Holy Quran contains guidelines and teachings for both individuals and society as a whole. The Holy Quran's guidelines and instructions for proper human conduct, a fair economic system, ritual worship, ethics and moral behavior, business, government, etc., are presented in this monumental text.

You are advised to read the instructional manual of life, the Holy Quran, and live as our Creator has commanded. How else would you know your role and the purpose of your existence unless you receive clear and practical instructions regarding God's expectations of you? If you follow the guidelines carefully, you shall be rewarded with a better life--now and in the hereafter. If you disobey God and go against His commands, by contrast, you will face the consequences in this world and the Hereafter.

The Holy Quran is the primary source of Islamic teachings for all Muslims. The Book is and always has been written in Arabic. The Holy Quran is so unique in content and style that it cannot be translated; therefore, any translation is only intended to interpret its meaning. Distinctions must be drawn between the Holy Quran and its translations.

Unlike other Scriptures of God, not one letter of the Holy Quran has been changed since its Revelation. Everything found in the Holy Quran is true, with no evidence of contradictions or falsehood found, and the truth of the book will remain valid for eternity.

Now let's review the irrefutable evidence that proves the Holy Quran to be the Word of God:

The Holy Quran is proof of Islam's truthfulness. Anyone who thoroughly examines the Holy Quran will conclude that no one, including the Prophet Muhammad PBUH, could have authored this Book, as no human could produce anything of its scope and magnitude. Thus, this text could come only from God.

13

The Holy Quran is the eternal miracle of the Prophet Muhamad PBUH, providing the truthfulness of his Prophethood. Past prophets performed miracles to prove their Prophethood, but all of these miracles ended with their deaths since they were Prophets meant to serve their people only. Since Prophet Muhammad, PBUH, is the last Prophet and meant to be followed till the end of time, his miracle needs to last for that duration so that the people who live after him can see his miracle and believe in his Prophethood. The Holy Quran remains preserved and exists today in the same form as it existed more than 1400 years ago.

The Holy Quran is the greatest miracle of God and contains thousands of miracles to prove its Godly origins. For a book to claim to be the word of God is a formidable statement indeed. Without clear evidence or with one contradiction found within the Book, the apparent Word of God would be proven false. The Holy Quran does not contain any contradictions, nor does it contain any information confirmed as incorrect.

THE HOLY QURAN'S QUALITY AND ELOQUENCE IS PROOF OF ITS DIVINE SOURCE

Now let's speak on the irrefutable proofs and evidence on why the Holy Quran is the true Speech of God. The Holy Quran will continue to speak to every generation until the Day of Judgment. Amongst the many miracles of the Holy Quran is the Quality and Eloquence of the Holy Quran when the text is read in Arabic. Arabic speakers can appreciate the linguistic perfection of the Arabic language of the Holy Quran—it stands as a living miracle of the Arabic language. The Arabs who lived at the time of Prophet Muhammad PBUH could appreciate the eloquence of the language of the Book as they spoke Arabic.

The Holy Quran contains the highest possible standard of rhetoric in its language, to the extent that it would be impossible for a human or group of humans to produce. The Holy Quran consists of perfect grammar. The Holy Quran explains complicated legal matters like inheritance in simple speech and imagery through the Arabic language. The Holy Quran is inimitable in style, form, and spiritual impact; the book's text has a unique rhythm, tone, rhyme, and genre like no other book. The Holy Quran uses terminology and descriptions that express a sophistication beyond what a 7th-century person living in the desert would know.

The Holy Quran contains many miracles that non-Arabic speakers can appreciate and recognize. The Holy Quran is a miracle because of the power the book wields over humans worldwide. Daily, it changes millions of lives and views. It transforms people into better human beings. The Holy Quran is a miracle because of its incredible spiritual power and positive psychological effects on those who read it. The Book often gives readers an indescribable feeling that moves them to tears, even if they do not speak or comprehend Arabic. The Holy Quran is a miracle, as it has changed and impacted human history in many ways.

The Holy Quran contains references to various branches of knowledge and various sciences that could not have been known firsthand at the time and place of the Prophet Muhammad PBUH and his companions. We will now dig a little deeper into this subject.

THE MANY SCIENTIFIC
MIRACLES OF THE HOLY QURAN

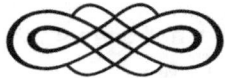

Among the many miracles of the Holy Quran are hundreds of scientific facts listed in the book, later confirmed to be accurate years after the Book was revealed. Whereas the Holy Quran contains accounts of hundreds of scientific miracles, it is not a book of science nor a book of engineering or medicine. The Holy Quran is a Book of Guidance containing spiritual signs that prove its divinity, coming from a higher power.

The Holy Quran was revealed to the Prophet Muhammad PBUH in the 7th century, an illiterate man living in the desert at a time when there were no telescopes, microscopes, or anything resembling the symbols of advanced technology we have today. As the faith in Islam continued to grow century after century, humanity evolved into the age of modern science. In this era, many scientific discoveries confirm references listed in certain verses of the Holy Quran. Of the many scientific miracles in the Quran, here are a few:

The Holy Quran addresses the evolution of the human embryo in the mother's womb in chronological order. Allah, the Glorious, uses a specific Arabic word to describe the embryo in the Holy

Quran: *Alaqah,* which translates to mean Blood Clot, suspended thing—that which hangs, a clinging substance, and a Leech. Allah calls the child in the womb *"that which hangs"* when even physicians did not know that a growing embryo hangs in the mother's womb.

The word *Alaqah* that God chose can translate to mean *blood clot* because the embryo's appearance and accompanying sacs seen during the alaqah stage are like those of a blood clot. The phrase *a suspended thing* can be used here because the embryo hangs in the mother's womb. Moreover, the word "leech" can be used because many similarities exist between an embryo and a leech. They appear identical and function similarly, as both obtain nourishment from the mother's blood. The three meanings of the word alaqah that God chose to apply here correspond accurately to the descriptions of the embryo at the alaqah stage.

"And certainly did We create man from an extract of clay. Then We placed him as a sperm-drop in a firm lodging. Then We made the sperm-drop into a clinging clot, and We made the clot into a lump of flesh, and We made from the lump, bones, and We covered the bones with flesh; then We developed him into another creation. So blessed is Allah, the best of creators."
(Quran 23:12-14)

The descriptions of embryology mentioned in the Holy Quran and Hadith agree with those revealed by the latest scientific discoveries in the field. These descriptions could not have been obtained based on the scientific knowledge available in the 7th century, proving that this knowledge could have come only from God. Moreover, God speaks of the embryo's three-stage growth process in the mother's womb. He reveals that He created the womb with three veils, cloaks, shields, or envelopes of darkness around the child. Now we know that three layers of darkness separate the embryo from the outside world.

Among the many miracles of the Holy Quran is God's statement that He created everything from water. It was not until later, after the invention of the microscope, that it was confirmed that every living thing consists primarily of water. We now know that all living things are made of cells, and these cells are made mostly of water.

"...and made from water every living thing?
Then will they not believe?" (Quran 21:30)

When God speaks of His creations in the Holy Quran, He uses the terms "He Created" or "We Created." For instance, God would state in the Holy Quran, *We created the Skies, the Earth, the Heavens, the Mountains,* etc. The "We" used here is the royal we; of course, this does not imply another Creator along with God, as there is only One Creator. When God references the element of iron in the Holy Quran, He states that *He sent down* as opposed to *created* iron.

Scientists later discovered that iron is not natural to the Earth's surface and was sent down from the galaxy. Geologists found that the Earth was struck by meteorites billions of years ago, with iron descending as the earthbound byproduct of exploding stars. Only God could have known this fact more than 1400 years ago.

"We have already sent Our messengers with clear evidence and
sent down with them the Scripture and the balance that the
people may maintain their affairs in justice. And We sent down
iron, wherein is great military might and benefits for the people,
and so that Allah may make evident those who support Him and
His messengers unseen. Indeed, Allah is Powerful and Exalted in
Might." (Quran 57:25)

Humans initially thought that the world was flat. The Holy Quran references the Earth in a verse using the word *dahaha,* a term derived from a word that explicitly describes the egg of an ostrich, which is geo-spherical in shape and akin to the exact shape of the Earth. Furthermore, the word *dahaha* also means *to expand* in Arabic. So, through the use of this word, God also tells us that the Earth is ever-expanding, a notion later confirmed to be true.

"And after that He spread the Earth." (Quran 79:30)

When people initially thought that the moon casts its own light, the Holy Quran references that the moon's light is not natural to this celestial being but instead takes the form of reflected light—a point that scientists have confirmed to be accurate. Yet another miracle of the Holy Quran!

"Blessed is He who has placed in the sky great stars and placed therein a burning lamp and luminous moon." (Quran 25:61)

Since the modern-day Bible is not the Word of God, this text states that the light of the moon is its own light: *And God made two great lights; the greater light to rule the day, and the lesser light to rule the night: he made the stars also. (Genesis 1:16)* However, modern science teaches us that the moon does not cast its own light. Since the Holy Quran is God's Word, it was in all ways correct; conversely, the Bible contains the words of men and has many errors!

The Holy Quran references the fact that God made mountains in the form of pegs. In this verse, the word used to refer to mountains is *aw'ta'da* in Arabic, which means pegs and stakes, much like those objects holding tents. Mountains provide the Earth's stability, preventing the planet from shaking, much like pegs offer stability to a tent. Like tent pegs, mountains bear deep roots embedded in the Earth.

"And He has cast into the Earth firmly set mountains, lest it shift with you, and made rivers and roads, that you may be guided." (Quran 15:15)

God mentions in a verse that the two seas come together on the face of the Earth without directly mixing. We now know that when two different seas meet, a barrier between them boasts its own salinity, temperature, and density. How can the Prophet Muhammad PBUH have

20

known this fact more than 1400 years ago in the desert when he never visited a place where saltwater ran? He had never visited an ocean. Prophet Muhammad PBUH had seen the sweet water of rivers and seas but never salt water.

"And it is He who has released simultaneously the two seas, one fresh and sweet and one salty and bitter, and He placed between them a barrier and prohibiting partition." (Quran 25:53)

Another miracle of the Holy Quran is an instance in which God references a dialogue of a queen ant, warning her community of dire happenings, saying, *O you ants! Get into your dwellings lest Solomon and his army crush you unawares.* We know that the animals whose life cycles bear the closest resemblance to our own are ants. They routinely meet and talk to each other in their nests, with the Queen Ants issuing instructions. They have within their home and population labor workers with supervisors, marketplaces where they exchange goods, and burial sites, just as we do.

"Until, when they came upon the valley of the ants, an ant said, 'O ants, enter your dwellings that you not be crushed by Solomon and his soldiers while they perceive not.' (Quran 27:18)

When the Prophet Muhammad PBUH was delivering the Message of God to the idol-worshippers of Mecca, most rejected his message and did not believe him. They demanded that he show a physical sign that he was indeed a Prophet of God. They wanted to see proof of His Prophethood by seeing the moon split in half—something a man cannot do without the help of God. Prophet Muhammad PBUH asked, "If I do as you requested, would you then believe that I am a Prophet sent by God and believe in the message of God?" They said yes! Heeding these words, Prophet Muhammad PBUH asked God to divide the moon as proof; He assented by splitting the moon in half and bringing it back together. Unfortunately, due to the arrogance of these idol-worshippers, many still did not believe in His Prophethood and message.

"The Hour of Judgment is nigh, and the moon is cleft asunder. And if they behold a portent they turn away and say: Prolonged illusion. They denied the truth and followed their own lusts. Yet everything will come to a decision." (Quran 54:1)

Today, through the wonders of modern technology, it has been proven through a picture captured by NASA that cracks do indeed line the moon's surface. NASA stated that the moon's two sides loomed separately at one time and then united. How did Prophet Muhammad PBUH know that the moon had split if this event did not occur? We have in our possession now the historical reports delivered by companions present at the time and even reports straight from enemies of Prophet Muhammad PBUH, who witnessed the event. We also have independent reports from people in other geographical locations, such as India, who witnessed it from their own particular vantage point. How did the Holy Quran convey more than 1400 years ago that the moon was a split element if the information did not come from God?

I outlined only a few of the many scientific miracles presented in the Holy Quran. An internet search will reveal the many others that exist. How could an illiterate man living in the desert possess such advanced knowledge at this historical time unless this knowledge came directly from above?

Prophecies and Predictions
of the Holy Quran

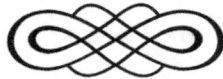

Linguistic and scientific wonders are not the only miracles conveyed through the Holy Quran, as it also contains prophecies that have since been realized. The Holy Quran provides many predictions related to future events. All of these Quranic predictions manifested as predicated.

Among the many accurate futuristic predictions made in these pages is the bold claim of the victory of the Byzantine Empire over the Persian Empire. In the early 7th century, the Byzantine and Persian empires were the two great global empires ruling and competing at the time. The Byzantines suffered a severe defeat in their fight against the Persians at the time, which seemed to doom the Empire. The Holy Quran stated that while the Byzantines did experience an initial loss during wartime, they would emerge victorious within three to nine years. They did indeed reign victorious, a fact that no one could have anticipated. God the Almighty states:

The Byzantines have been defeated. In the nearest land. But they, after their defeat, will overcome. Within three to nine years. To Allah belongs the command before and after. And that day the believers will rejoice. In the victory of Allah. He gives victory to whom He wills, and He is the Exalted in Might, the Merciful. (Quran 30-2-5)

Not only did this prediction come to fruition, but this verse referenced the fact that, in geographic terms and as conveyed in the Arabic language, the Romans were defeated *in the lowest land.* We later came to find via modern satellite images that the location of their defeat is indeed the lowest point on the face of the Earth. This vicinity boasted the lowest altitude on Earth, 400 meters below sea level.

The Pharaoh, who lived in the time of Prophet Moses PBUH, had power and wealth; he even arrogantly proclaimed himself to be God. He eventually drowned; his fate stood as a direct punishment for his arrogance. In a verse of the Holy Quran, God stated that He would preserve the Pharaoh's body as a sign for those who came after him. His body was discovered in 1898.

In the early '70s, his corpse was examined. It was discovered through intense investigation of his mummy that he had died from direct water infiltration into his lung, providing conclusive proof of a drowning death. It also was proven that he lived at the time of the Prophet Moses PBUH. God preserved his body forever as a sign and lesson for humanity, as He had promised in His Final Revelation. This body is displayed in a museum and often tours the world for everyone to see.

"So today We will save you in body that you may be to those who succeed you a sign. And indeed, many among the people, of Our signs, are heedless." (Quran 10:92)

After the idol-worshippers forced Prophet Muhammad PBUH and the Muslims to flee the Holy land of Mecca, they settled in the city of

Medina. These idol-worshippers continued prosecuting the Muslims and tried to cease the spread of the Message of Islam. The Holy Quran stated that Muslims would re-enter the Sacred House of Allah, Mecca, victoriously in a state of security. This prediction was realized in the eighth year of the Hijrah, with Muslims going forth with their hair shaved or cut short. As the verse states, they performed a pilgrimage and fulfilled the rituals without fear.

"Indeed, Allah has made true to His Messenger the dream shown with truth: You will definitely enter the Sacred Mosque inshā'allāh (if Allah wills,) peacefully, with your heads shaved, and your hairs cut short, having no fear. So He knew what you did not know, and He assigned before that a victory, near at hand." (Quran 48:27)

Many other prophecies fill the Holy Quran; for instance, God's claim that He would safeguard and protect his final Book to humanity, the Holy Quran, from human-made alterations or any form of corruption. As stated in a previous chapter, the Holy Quran remains the same way it arrived, letter by letter.

"Indeed, it is We who sent down the message [i.e., the Quran], and indeed, We will be its guardian." (Quran 15:9)

The Holy Quran also contains God's claim that He rendered the Holy Quran easy to memorize; today, hundreds of thousands of people have memorized the entire Book, which contains more than 600 pages. Millions of people have memorized the text, regardless of their ethnicity and language. This is the only Book on Earth that is easy to memorize.

"And indeed We have already made the Quran easy for remembrance. Are there any that will recollect?" (Quran 54:17)

Prophet Muhammad PBUH's Predictions From Hadith All Came True

N ot only does the Holy Quran give prophecies for the future, but the prophetic sayings of Prophet Muhammad PBUH also have conveyed many predictions. We can outline a few among the more than 100 prophecies in the Hadith of Prophet Muhammad PBUH (sayings of the Prophet).

When Arab pagans were not known for building tall buildings, as the Romans, Greeks, and Egyptians were, the Prophet Muhammad PBUH prophesied a time when you would see the children of barefooted camel and goat herders participating in the construction of high-rise buildings. He pointed out that this would signify the onset of Judgment Day.

This prophecy was made at a time and place when no indications existed that Arabs would construct tall buildings; indeed, this was at a time when Arabs lived as impoverished herders of camels and sheep. The fathers of the current rulers of Dubai and Saudi Arabia once walked barefoot and worked primarily as herders of camels and goats before discovering oil. Today, Dubai and Saudi Arabia host the world's tallest buildings. ...*And when you see barefoot, naked, destitute shepherds constructing tall buildings...* - Saheeh Muslim.

The Prophet Muhammad PBUH also predicted that Jerusalem would be conquered after his death, lost, and then conquered once again. He prophesied the conquest of Persia, Rome, and Egypt. Muslims conquered Constantinople (modern-day Istanbul) after his death, as predicted. Prophet Muhammad PBUH predicted that Islam would spread to the far Eastern and Western ends of the world. Now we see that Islam has spread worldwide, encompassing 24% of the world's population.

Among the many predictions of Prophet Muhammad PBUH is the claim that a time would come when ...*women are clothed yet naked, walking with an enticing gait...* (narrated by Ahmad & Muslim in Al-Saheeh). Today, women worldwide walk in the streets with many body parts exposed, flaunting their beauty as the Hadith predicted.

Prophet Muhammed PBUH prophesied a time when murders would increase, and the one who kills would not know why they killed, nor would the one killed understand the motive. One can see this phenomenon happening in modern wars and gang-related conflicts.

Prophet Muhammed PBUH prophesied the increase in usury and interest, acts which are unethical and exploitative as they make the rich richer at the expense of the poor. He stated that no one would be able to escape this state, which, unfortunately, defines the world's current economic conditions.

Prophet Muhammad PBUH ordered Mosques (houses of God) to be built with a design of pure simplicity. He prophesied a time when Mosques would be like palaces, and now, we see many huge, beautiful Mosques worldwide just brimming with pillars, chandeliers, domes, beautiful colored carpets, and marbled floors.

MIRACLES OF THE HOLY QURAN AND KNOWLEDGE OF PAST EVENTS

Not only does the Holy Quran prophesize future events, but the text tells many stories of past events, past nations, and past prophets, such as the stories of Prophet Joseph, Moses, and Jesus PBUT. The Prophet Muhammad PBUH lived in the middle of the desert with no libraries available because the Arabian Peninsula was a backward, antiquated nation at the time. He was unlettered and grew up among illiterate idol worshippers without knowledge of the Scriptures. He had no way of reading or conjuring these stories shared in the Holy Quan.

"That is from the news of the unseen which We reveal to you, [O Muhammad]. You knew it not, neither you nor your people, before this. So be patient; indeed, the [best] outcome is for the righteous." (Quran 11:49)

Mathematical Miracles
in the Holy Quran

G od taught the Holy Quran to the Angel Gabriel, who then
taught it to the Prophet Muhammad PBUH, who then taught
it to his companions. It is imperative to know that Muslims
recorded the Revelation as it was taught to them by Prophet Muhammad
PBUH over 23 years. The Holy Quran was revealed passage by passage
orally. It did not come down in written form. After the Book was
compiled, it was apparent that the Holy Quran consisted of a deep
mathematical structure and design that only God could have achieved.
The Holy Quran contains many mathematical miracles or presumed
coincidences that cannot be mere coincidences.

Among the many mathematical miracles outlined in the Holy Quran
is the mention of the word *day* 365 times, which is the time it takes the
Earth to complete a single orbit around the sun. The plural of the word
is used 30 times within the text, representing the number of days in a
typical month. The word *month* is used 12 times in this same text. The
words, *man* and *woman* are mentioned 24 times each, and sometimes in
different contexts. The word *Dunya* (the world we live in) is mentioned
115 times, and the word that references the Hereafter is mentioned 115
times.

Again, God did not reveal the Holy Quran entirely at once; it was revealed to the Prophet Muhammad PBUH through Angel Gabriel orally, piece by piece, over 23 years. A human could never compile the Holy Quran, brimming with a bounty of mathematical miracles, in 23 years. These are only a few of the many miracles found in the Holy Quran. These miracles, along with many others found in the text, show a deliberate order in the Holy Quran. All of the presumed mathematical coincidences cannot be, in fact, coincidences.

Unlike the modern-day Bible, which contains thousands of contradictions due to its excessive modifications and insertions from human hands, the Holy Quran boasts perfect consistency and contains zero contradictions, even though this more than 600-page Book speaks of many complex topics such as theology, law, legal problems, peace and war, marriage and divorce, economics, child custody, inheritance, etc. God states that if this Book were written by anyone else, the text undoubtedly would contain many contradictions.

Given the fact that Prophet Muhammad PBUH was an unlettered man who did not know how to read or write and lived in the desert, he could not have authored the Holy Quran as it is written, at a high literacy level of the Arabic language, containing no errors, contradictions, nor inconsistencies.

"Then do they not reflect upon the Qur'an? If it had been from any other than Allah, they would have found within it much contradiction." (Quran 4:82)

The Holy Quran contains perfect consistency and is free of contradictions, even though it was revealed orally over twenty-three years. The Holy Quran challenges anyone who doubts the Book's Divine origins to produce another sacred text equal in merit, one that matches its eloquence, power, style, language, etc. Allah made it clear that no one will be able to produce anything comparable to the Holy Quran— another prophecy of the Holy Quran that is true.

"And if you are in doubt about what We have sent down upon Our Servant [Muhammad], then produce a surah the like thereof and call upon your witnesses other than Allah, if you should be truthful." (Quran 2:23)

WHAT IS LIFE'S PURPOSE, AND WHY SHOULD YOU CONVERT TO ISLAM?

If you do not have a relationship with your Creator, then your soul eternally will seek something to fill the emptiness of your heart. All of the wealth and material goods of this world never will fill the void, the emptiness, the gap of your vacant soul. Your happiness is not derived from the gathering of possessions. Real wealth is obtained only from the richness and contentment of the heart and soul. And the only true poverty is the poverty of your spirit and heart. Whether you believe it or not, whether you like it or not, this is how God designed you and how He designed the world you live in.

In today's materialistic world, the endless quest for fame and wealth distracts you from reflecting on the beautiful creation of God and the purpose behind it. You live in a world where people are obsessed with materialism; their main aim and focus is to gather all the money and prizes they can possess. You are in a world in which people are obsessed with taking as much as possible from this world. A perpetual state of excessive materialism can affect your inner peace. You cannot achieve satisfaction in life if you do little but pursue material gain to an excessive and extreme extent; instead, you should look at the situation of those less fortunate than you. This way, you will have a greater appreciation of the love, gifts, benefits, and mercy the Almighty has bestowed upon you regarding your wealth, family, friends, housing, etc.

You were created and born with a sense of awe and wonder, but many kill that sense of wonder somewhere along their journey to adulthood. Many no longer feel awe at God's creation around them because of their excessiveness, obsession, and distraction as rooted in the material things of this world. Many are so preoccupied with useless material goods, vain talk, and gossip that they have forgotten and even are immune to the wonder of the miracles happening around them every second of every day. One should think deeply and ask more critical questions about life and its purpose rather than thinking about that which is less significant.

For the few that ponder and think deeply on this creation, which others overlook, they discover within it signs and great lessons all around them that lead them straight back to their Creator. Signs that lead one to an appreciation of the Wisdom and Wonders of the Almighty's creation, bringing them thus closer to their Lord. In the Holy Quran, God invites individuals of true understanding to think about the issues other people overlook.

You surely harbor fundamental questions that malign your conscience. Why was I created? What am I doing here? What is the purpose of my existence? Where am I headed? These are questions that only God can answer. Only He can provide you with a meaningful purpose for your life and the guidance needed to fulfill your life's purpose.

Other religions do not answer the big questions of life. You cannot live peacefully in this world without knowing who you are, who created you, where you are headed, what your role is, and how to fulfill that role. The Almighty implanted the need to answer these questions into your inner nature. However, your human intellect alone cannot answer these questions unaided. You need Divine guidance to discover these all-important spiritual answers.

The answers lie in Islam.

The brightest and most significant thinkers of the past never would deny the various signs that point to the existence of their Creator. However, the element that led many people of the past astray was their lack of knowing God to the truest extent and the fact that they did not have access to a true and preserved Revelation originating from God. Addressing the ones that deny God's existence, God poses an argument in the Quran, stating:

"...Or were they created by nothing, or are they their own creators?" (Quran 52:35)

The Holy Quran teaches you that the signs and proofs of God's knowledge, Wisdom, Power, Mercy, and existence are evident in the world around you. Together they point to a Creator, a Maker, a Designer, and a Fashioner. This creation is flawless and perfect. Life on Earth and the Universe itself demonstrates so much order, purpose, intelligence, and design, all of which prove the existence of a Creator that designed and fashioned everything.

Thus, God calls you to ponder, reflect, and think deeply about the design of this complex creation to build a better understanding of Him. When you reflect, you realize that this world and everything it contains was created with intelligence and Infinite Wisdom—not by chance. Allah refers to the Earth, the Sun, the Moon, the merging of the night into the day, and the merging of the Day into Night, as His miraculous signs and evidence of the existence of a Creator. God states that the skies and the Earth are fashioned perfectly, showing proof they originated from the act of a Creator.

"Indeed, in the creation of the heavens and earth, and the alternation of the night and the day, and the great ships which sail through the sea with that which benefits people, and what Allah has sent down from the heavens of rain, giving life thereby to the earth after its lifelessness and dispersing therein every kind of moving creature, and His directing of the winds and the clouds controlled between the heaven and the earth are signs for a people who use reason." (Quran 2:164)

God asks you to reflect upon the Mountains, the Sun, the Moon, the Stars, the Trees, etc. so that you realize the value and extent of your blessings. You will witness a clear sign, evidence, and proof of His existence, as you look up to the sky and admire the beauty of the ocean, mountain, and sunset:

Have they not looked at the Heaven above them - how We structured it and adorned it and how it has no rifts? (Quran 50:6)

The miracles of nature, the Earth, and the Universe are enough evidence to show you that there exists something bigger than us. You do not need to see anything more from God to believe; the world is already enough of a miracle and sufficient proof of His power. God also encourages you to look at your own self, your body, and how it was constructed so perfectly to see additional proof.

"We will show them Our signs in the horizons and within themselves until it becomes clear to them that it is the truth. But is it not sufficient concerning your Lord that He is, over all things, a Witness?" (Quran 41:53)

Pondering over the creation of humanity and the Universe would help you realize that the Deity behind this ethereal creation can re-create it once again. You would understand that God can resurrect you and all of humanity with ease in anticipation of Judgement Day.

"How can you disbelieve in Allah when you were lifeless, and He brought you to life; then He will cause you to die, then He will bring you back to life, and then to Him, you will be returned."
(Quran 2:28)

God the Almighty, due to his abundant Love and Mercy for humanity, has not left you in pure darkness, leaving you alone and unenlightened to stumble your way down the right path with only the frailties of guesswork or trial and error to aid you. God gifted you with an intellect and a logical mind that can reason, ponder, and reflect. God gave you the gift of Divine Guidance, which outlines the Criterion for ultimate truth and knowledge.

You must use your intellect and reason to contemplate and recognize God's signs and evidence of His wonder, build a relationship with Him, and follow His guidance. These signs serve to speak loudly in their impact and evidence, giving you the information you need.

The disbelievers, the rejecters of the truth, the deniers of God, will live a narrow, depressed life in this world and suffer in hellfire forever in the hereafter.

"And whoever turns away from My remembrance - indeed, he will have a depressed life, and We will gather him on the Day of Resurrection blind." (Quran 20:124)

Humans can't navigate the twists and turns of this life without God's Guidance. Humans must ask their Creator for guidance. God bestowed Guidance unto His servants in the form of Revelation and through prayer, the form of communication through which Muslims connect with God at least five times a day. Your goal as a follower of Islam is to become a faithful servant of God by submitting to His Will and worshiping Him Alone. Those who pass this test would enter Paradise eternally; those who fail would enter hellfire in the afterlife. Remember that Judgment Day is a blink away. You will live and die, and then you will be resurrected to face your Lord, who will judge you based on how you lived your life.

"...Indeed, we belong to Allah, and indeed to Him, we will return." (Quran 2:156)

The Religion of Islam states that God forces no one to submit to His Will. He has laid out a clear path for you while making it known that you must choose from two routes: The straight path that leads to Heaven or the erroneous way, which leads to hell. You are free to make your own choices. If you worship God, pledge your devotion to Him, and obey His commands, you have grasped and achieved the firm handhold and eternal bond that never will break. But if you deny God's existence or worship anyone other than Allah, you stand to face eternal punishment in the hereafter.

Your life purpose has been given to you by your Creator. He has sent it down to you via the power of Revelation via your Prophet. Your life's purpose is to find God, build a relationship with Him, and continuously submit to His will. The best joy and peace you can achieve in this world will be derived from servitude to your Creator. You must try to be an obedient slave of God. God states unequivocally that humankind was created to worship Him. God states:

"And I did not create the jinn and mankind except to worship Me." (Quran 51:56)

You could misunderstand this to mean that God wants you to exist in a constant state of prayer, dwell on the remembrance of Him at all times, and spend your entire life in a state of constant seclusion and absolute meditation. This is not the case. In Islam, worshipping God includes and entails every act, belief, statement, or sentiment of the heart, which God approves and loves. The act of worship in Islam is comprehensive in scope.

The worship of God can include actions such as removing an object from the road, helping one in need, being kind to your parents, lawfully making money, sharing food with neighbors, visiting an ill person, etc. The act must be done sincerely to please your Creator and not with boastful or impure motives. The action also should be consistent with the Almighty's guidance and laws. Any thought or act that brings a person closer to his Creator would be considered an act of worship.

To worship God is to get to know Him, learn His Names and attributes, love Him, obey His commandments, and enforce His laws in every aspect of your life. To worship God is to serve His cause, engage in the struggle and quest to do right, shun evil, and be just to others. Obeying God's commandments and refraining from prohibited activities would make your life easier and more comfortable and lighten your burdens.

"And Allah wants to lighten for you your burden/ difficulties, and mankind was created weak." (Quran 4:28)

God created you to be a follower and a worshipper. If you are not devoted to God, you instead will devote yourself to others, whether they are false gods, saints, idols, philosophers, etc., following them by committing thoughts and actions that would lead you astray. Muslims do not worship the creations of God, such as the Sun, the Moon, or an idol; instead, they worship the Creator Himself. Islam recognizes that God has created you with an innate eagerness and ability to seek God, to acknowledge and understand the existence of your Creator.

You may believe through error that disobeying the commands of God, all the while partying your whole life away, would make for a more enjoyable, peaceful life. You may think that if you find God and follow His commands, you will deprive yourself of things you could otherwise have enjoyed—and this couldn't be further from the truth. Quite the opposite is true. While the commands of other religions often are viewed as burdensome and rigid, the rules of Islam are not seen in this way by

38

the devout Muslim. Devout Muslims see these rules as guidelines to indicate as to what's best for them so that they may be guided to success, happiness, honor, and contentment in this life and the next.

God states that if you abide by His commands, He will relieve your life's burdens, rendering your existence much easier, more comfortable, and more relaxed. You would find contentment in your heart. You would find more peace and harmony within yourself and with the things and people around you. Each of God's commandments is enforced to benefit the one that follows them. Anything that God renders impermissible is harmful to oneself or society. For example, alcohol is prohibited in Islam because of its danger and evilness. Many studies and evidence demonstrate the effects and risks of drinking alcohol. Those who follow these simple edicts will enjoy a pleasant, contented life in a blessed world. God promises in the Holy Quran:

"Whoever does righteousness, whether male or female, while he is a believer - We will surely cause him to live a good life, and We will surely give them their reward in the Hereafter according to the best of what they used to do." (Quran 16:97)

God created desires within the human being. You can control these desires in accordance with God's Law and live decently, or succumb to them and go astray. Allah, the Glorious, created you with the knowledge that you would sin. Therefore, God taught humans, starting with Prophet Adam, peace be upon him, how to repent and purify oneself of sin.

Life in this world is also a test for humankind. Everyone faces a separate and unique test. Some are tested when they attempt to endure a life of poverty; some are tempted by wealth, some enjoy good health, some suffer bad health, etc. God states in his Holy Book:

"He who created death and life to test you as to which of you is best in deeds - and He is the Exalted in Might, the Forgiving." (Quran 67:2)

At times, the Almighty tests His creation through calamities and sometimes blessings to discover who will respond by being thankful and ungrateful, who will obey, and who will disobey.

"And We will surely test you with something of fear and hunger and a loss of wealth and lives and fruits, but give good tidings to the patient" (Quran 2:155)

God tests all of humanity in different ways. God is testing every individual every day. You should not mistake your life problems for punishments or as signs that God is displeased with you. Likewise, you should never interpret your wealth, provisions, rewards, luxuries, and pleasures as signs that Allah is pleased with you or that you are privileged. Sometimes, quite the opposite is true. Allah also says:

"Know that your wealth and your children are but a trial and that Allah has with Him a mighty reward." (Quran 8:28)

God, in His Wisdom and Mercy, has decreed that people be tried and tested in various ways to develop their psyches and strengthen and improve their character. Sometimes when you undergo certain instances of suffering, you immediately think about and pray to God in response, even if you are not religious. At times, the very experience of suffering leads one to God.

A Muslim views this world as a temporary stop en route to a final destination: the afterlife, where you will live eternally. Not that this temporary world is unimportant or should be taken lightly, but this life should not be lived sinfully at the expense of the Hereafter—which is much longer and better in scope. If your goal in life is to become wealthy, then you will have no purpose in existence after you achieve the goal of wealth. How, then, could wealth be considered the aim of life? This world is not about acquiring material goods or physical pleasures.

A Muslim views and interacts with this world for that which it is, just a means to an end. The act of detaching from this world doesn't mean that you abandon all material possessions and own nothing substantial; on the contrary, a healthy detachment from this world means that nothing can hold, own, and enslave you. This life is about attaining a higher purpose. One should spend their time on Earth preparing for the eternal joy of the afterlife. The purpose of life in Islam is to become faithful, sincere servants of God.

"And this worldly life is not but diversion and amusement. And indeed, the home of the Hereafter - that is the eternal life, if only they knew." (Quran 29:64)

This life is temporary and will end someday for you; another day will bring an end for humanity altogether. But the Hereafter is eternal. The experience of life in this world is insubstantial when compared to life in the Hereafter. Prophet Muhammad, peace be upon him, stated: *What is the example of this worldly life compared to the Hereafter other than one of you dipping his finger in the sea? Let him see what he brings forth.*

Whereas the essential purpose for which humankind was created is embodied in the worship of God, God does not need human worship. He certainly did not create you out of a need to seek His Glory. If not a single person worshipped God, His Glory would not diminish. God exists with no needs. On the other hand, you were created with needs and wants. Thus, it is you that requires the worship of God. You need to worship and glorify God by obeying his divinely revealed laws; obedience to God is the key to success in this life and the Hereafter.

You are encouraged to remember God as often as possible for your benefit. Remembrance of God is imperative, as sin is generally committed when God is forgotten. The forces of evil operate most freely when cognizance of God is weak or lost.

"Satan has overcome them and made them forget the remembrance of Allah. Those are the party of Satan. Unquestionably, the party of Satan - they will be the losers." (Quran 58:19)

Satan and his children seek to occupy your mind with irrelevant thoughts, material distractions, and desires that make you forget your Lord.

"O, believers! Remember God often." (Quran 33:41)

Everything in nature functions according to fixed laws set forth by God and cannot deviate from those laws. The Sun knows its role. It knows the cycle of its rotation; it knows its role as the giver of light, heat, and energy on Earth. The Earth knows its rotation cycle around its axis. Your eyes, heart, brain, body, and all of their components are subject to the laws of nature and have no choice but to operate as intended.

God's creation worships Him in a manner appropriate to their situation. The Sun, the Moon, the Stars, the Mountains, the trees, the animals, and the whole Universe all exist in a state of subjugation to Allah, the Almighty. All of them worshipping Him in an appropriate manner. God's creation prostrates to Him as per their nature, even if they do not press their foreheads to the ground. Man is expected to worship and praise his Creator, much like the surrounding creations continuously praise God in humility. God, the Almighty, said:

"Do you not see that to Allah prostrates whoever is in the Heavens and whoever is on the Earth and the Sun, the Moon, the Stars, the Mountains, the trees, the moving creatures and many of the people? But upon many, the punishment has been justified. And he whom Allah humiliates - for him there is no bestower of honor. Indeed, Allah does what He wills." (Quran 22:18)

"The seven heavens and the Earth and whatever is in them exalt Him. And there is not a thing except that it exalts Allah by His praise, but you do not understand their way of exalting. Indeed, He is ever Forbearing and Forgiving." (Quran 17:44)

You are expected to worship and praise your Creator, much like the surrounding creations continuously praise God in humility. All of God's creations know their mission and purpose. Just like the physical world submits to its Lord, human beings must submit to the Will and Laws of God. Unlike other creations of God, you were gifted with intelligence, the ability to comprehend and understand, and the wisdom to think, reflect, and ponder your Creator and your life purpose. You were gifted with the ultimate beauty of expression and the ability to make choices and decisions. God created many astounding creations, and the noblest of those creations are human beings. God states in the Quran:

**"We have certainly created man in the best of stature."
(Quran 95:4)**

You face a choice: the offer to submit before God like all other creations and be in harmony with everything else around you, or to go astray and violate God's laws. All will be held accountable for their decisions and choices.

**"To Him submits whatever is in the Heavens and the Earth."
(Quran 3:83)**

**"Glorify the praises of your Lord and be of those
who prostrate to Him." (Quran 15:98)**

You were born with an innate eagerness and ability to seek God and recognize and understand your Creator's existence. Once many discover the truth, they hasten to submit to Allah, entering a state of total submission—you should follow their lead.

You were born in a pure and pristine original state that inclines toward that which is ethical, morally, spiritually pure, upright, and wholesome. You are naturally inclined to help others, remove objects from the road, thank people when you are helped, etc. You have an internal moral conscience, a calculator, and a compass built into your being. If your being is not corrupted, your intrinsic moral conscience suffers discomfort and is disturbed when someone does wrong. This conscience always points toward good, which brings one closer to God. This goodness, programmed in you and all humans, compels you to be grateful when something good comes your way.

You have the instinct to believe in and worship your Creator, who is One—and who has no partners. This belief does not come about as a result of learning or personal reflection but is placed by God into the heart of every human. With time, the changing environment, and the outside influences from parents and friends, this innate belief in God affects and confuses some people at first. Prophet Muhammad, peace be upon him, narrated: *Every child is born in a state of fitrah (a natural belief in God), then his parents make him a Jew, a Christian, or a Magian. (Saheeh Muslim).*

May your journey to the answer and the truth be pleasant and successful.

The Sincere Seeker's Introductory book to Islam,

'*The Sacred Path to Islam*,' and other Islamic books for adults and children are available on The Sincere Seeker's Amazon page: www.amazon.com/thesincereseeker

You are encouraged to visit and subscribe to The Sincere Seeker's Blog at www.TheSincereSeeker.com and

The Sincere Seeker's YouTube Channel: www.YouTube.com/c/TheSincereSeeker

For questions or comments, please contact me at: hello@thesincereseeker.com

Ready to submit to your Creator?

You can convert to Islam and become Muslim in a 5-min Call with me.

Schedule your call here: https://www.thesincereseeker.com/convert-to-islam-and-become-muslim/

www.ingramcontent.com/pod-product-compliance
Lightning Source LLC
Chambersburg PA
CBHW061326120626
46546CB00007B/2700

* 9 7 8 1 9 5 8 3 1 3 7 6 3 *